The Summer

Chapter 1: A Challenge .... page 2

Chapter 2: At the Fete .... page 8

Chapter 3: The Cake Problem .... page 16

Chapter 4: Where's Dennis? .... page 20

Chapter 5: The Winner .... page 25

Written by Adam and Charlotte Guillain

Chapter 1: A Challenge

It was the end of the school year.

"I'm giving you all a challenge for the holidays," said Mrs Knight, as she handed out plastic folders to everyone. "Each of these folders has six pockets. I want you all to collect six things that tell the story of your summer."

The classroom came alive with chatter. Rav put up his hand. "What sort of things do you mean?" he asked.

"You could collect things you find or souvenirs you buy on days out," said Mrs Knight. "Or it could be something you've made. It's completely up to you!"

Everyone started talking, so Mrs Knight clapped her hands.

"Now we need to think about Saturday's school fete!" she announced. "Can you think of any good ideas to raise money?"

Finn put up his hand. "I could have a beat the goalie stand," he said. "I just need a goal and a football!"

"Lovely," said Mrs Knight.

Summer Fete

"Could we have remote controlled car races?" asked Rav.

"Great idea," said Mrs Knight. Rav beamed and asked Chris to help him.

Tess and Asha had been huddled together whispering.
"Can we do a guess the weight of the cake stall?" asked Tess.

"Yes, that sounds perfect!" said their teacher.

After school on Friday, Asha went to Tess's flat to make the cake.

"It needs to be big," said Tess with a grin.

They made two sponge cakes and sandwiched them together with jam. Then they covered the cake in pink icing.

"I brought these animal decorations to put on top," said Asha.

"Brilliant," said Tess, as Asha put a bear and a rabbit on top of the cake. They stood back to admire it.

"We'd better weigh it!" said Tess, reaching for the scales.

Asha wrote down the weight. "One kilogram and 637 grams!" she said. "Don't tell anyone!"

Chapter 2: At the Fete

The next morning, Tess's Dad carefully carried their cake to school and Mrs Knight put it in the staffroom while everyone set up their stalls.

"Can you help me measure this?" called Finn to Asha. She ran over to help.

"I need to mark the spot to place the ball," said Finn. Asha held the measuring tape on the goal line and Finn measured four metres outwards. "Thanks!" he called.

Tess helped Rav and Chris set up their car race. When the fete was about to start, Mrs Knight brought out the cake.

The fete was soon busy. Lots of people crowded around the stalls.

"Guess the weight of the cake!" called Tess loudly. "It's only a pound a go!"

Rav's mum came over. "One kilogram and 754 grams!" she said, and Asha wrote down her guess.

Guess the Weight
of the Cake

A voice on the loudspeaker announced, "The dance display will start in five minutes!"

"We're in that!" said Asha.

"What about our stall?" asked Tess with a frown.

Asha grabbed a piece of paper and wrote 'Back in fifteen minutes' on it. "Come on!" she cried, running off into the school.

Guess the Weight of the Cake

Asha and Tess were just in time for the dance display.
Tess waved to her parents as the music started, then she linked
arms with Asha and spun around.

"Which way now?" whispered Asha, as they bumped into two
girls. "Sorry!" she whispered.

"Follow Sophie!" called Tess, trying not to giggle.

The girls finished the dance with a cartwheel and the audience clapped and cheered.

"Well done, Asha!" called her dad from the back of the crowd.

"Quick, let's get back to our stall," said Tess, pulling Asha's arm. Together, they ran across the field, panting and laughing.

But as they ran up to the table, Tess and Asha stopped in their tracks and gasped.

"Our cake!" wailed Tess.

"W-what happened?" stammered Asha, tears welling in her eyes.

A huge chunk was missing from their beautiful cake!

Back in fifteen minutes

Guess the Weight of the Cake

Tess and Asha stood by the table and stared. Chunks of icing and crumbs were scattered to one side and they could hear a chomping noise under the table. They crouched down and peered under the cloth. A little dog was munching on the missing chunk of their cake!

Chapter 3: The Cake Problem

"Hey!" shouted Tess. The dog looked up and bolted across the field, leaving crumbs behind him.

"What are we going to do now?" asked Asha, as they stood up and stared at the remains of the cake left on the plate.

"We could get another cake from the cake stall over there?" suggested Tess.

Guess th of th

But there were only a couple of muffins left.

"The cakes were very popular!" Mrs Knight told them. "Has anyone guessed the weight of your cake correctly yet?"

"Um, not yet," said Tess, pulling Asha away.

"We need to think of something," said Asha. "We can't let Mrs Knight down!"

Guess the Weight of the Cake

As they covered up the remains of their cake, a woman holding a dog lead and a big pink teddy came hurrying over.

"You haven't seen a little brown dog, have you?" she asked the girls. "I've lost him."

Asha frowned but Tess nudged her and whispered, "She looks worried. Don't mention the cake."

The woman was glancing around anxiously.

"We saw him earlier," Tess told her. "We'll help you look for him."

"Thank you!" said the woman. "I'm Emma and he's called Dennis!"

The three of them set off to search the fete.

Chapter 4: Where's Dennis?

Tess ran to look behind the pizza van while Asha checked the tombola stall.

"He's not at the bouncy castle!" shouted Emma.

"There's Rav. Have you seen a little dog?" Asha called to him.

Rav nodded as they ran over. "He was here," he said, raising his eyebrows. "Chasing the cars!"

"Which way did he go?" asked Emma, scanning the crowd.

"That way," said Rav, pointing up the field.

"I hope he didn't run out on to the road," Tess whispered to Asha as they followed Emma. Then they heard a loud shout.

Hey! Stop it!

"That's Finn!" cried Asha, changing direction and sprinting towards the beat the goalie stand.

Finn was waving his arms and chasing a small brown dog, who was playing with his football.

"Dennis!" shouted Emma.

She hurried over and put Dennis on his lead. "How can I thank you for helping me?" she asked.

"Well, there is something we need help with …"
said Asha, sighing.

They led Emma to their stall and showed her the half-eaten cake. Emma looked at the crumbs on Dennis's nose and put a hand over her mouth.

"I'm so sorry!" she whispered.

"Can I buy you a replacement cake?" Emma suggested.

"Thanks, but there aren't any left," said Tess, bending down to pat Dennis. Then Tess looked up with a glint in her eyes.

"I've got an idea," she said with a giggle. She whispered in Asha's ear.

"What is it?" asked Emma.

Chapter 5: The Winner

Asha grabbed a big blue marker and crossed out the word 'Cake' on their sign. Then she wrote the word 'Dog' in its place.

Emma lifted Dennis up on to the table and said, "Sit!" very firmly.

Tess started to shout, "Guess the weight of the dog! Only a pound a go!"

Sophie wandered over and tilted her head on one side as she stroked Dennis.

"Do we win the dog if we guess right?" she asked, her eyes wide.

"Oh!" gasped Tess, glancing at Emma.

"Don't worry," said Emma, laughing. "This can be the prize." She held up the pink teddy she'd won in the tombola.

Soon a crowd had gathered around their stall and the jar of pound coins was filling up. Mrs Knight came across to have a go.

"Now let me see that cake," she called, pulling out her purse. "Oh!"

"We had a change of plan," Asha told her with a grin.

Mrs Knight guessed Dennis's weight and looked at her watch.

"You'd better weigh him now," she said. "The fete's almost over."

Emma lifted Dennis on to the scales gently.

"He's six kilograms exactly!" shouted Tess. "Rav is the winner!"

Rav went red. "I'm a bit too old for pink teddies," he said, and handed it to Alpa.

"We raised a lot of money in the end," said Asha, holding up the jar of coins.

Meanwhile, Tess was picking the bear and rabbit decorations off the remains of the cake. "And we can use these for our holiday challenge!" she said with a grin.

The Summer Fete

What other things will the Comet Street Kids collect for their holiday challenge? Read the other books in this band to find out!

The Summer Fete

At the Seaside

The Laughing Kookaburra

Help the Vikings

The Sleepover

Asteroid Alarm!

Talk about the story

Answer the questions:

1 What did Mrs Knight ask the class to do at the beginning of the story?

2 What sort of stand did Finn decide to have at the fete?

3 What decorations did Tess and Asha put on top of the cake?

4 What does the word 'display' mean? Can you think of another word that means the same thing?

5 Why did Tess and Asha leave a note on their stall?

6 Why was Finn chasing the dog?

7 Describe what the dog did in your own words.

8 What stall would you like to run at a school fete?

Can you retell the story using your own words?